Waiting for the Snow

Copyright © 2021 Deborah Hochberg

All world rights reserved.

No part of this book may be reproduced, stored in a retrieval system, or transmitted in any form or by any means electronic, mechanical, photocopying, recording or otherwise, without the prior consent of the publisher.

Readers are encouraged to go to MissionPointPress.com to contact the author or to find information on how to buy this book in bulk at a discounted rate.

Published by Mission Point Press
2554 Chandler Road
Traverse City, MI 49696
(231) 421-9513

MissionPointPress.com

Cover photo: "Wind Tree" by Deborah Hochberg

ISBN: 978-1-950659-96-8

Library of Congress Control Number: 2021900946

Printed in the United States of America

Waiting for the Snow

POEMS

Deborah Hochberg

MISSION POINT PRESS

*Dedicated to my father Israel Hochberg.
May his memory be a blessing.*

Contents

Hot Tea On A Summer Night	1
Waiting	2
A Book	4
Evening Sky	5
Cass Corridor Bar	6
The Bartender	8
Evening Conversation	9
A Night On The Town	10
D.L.	12
Halloween Night	13
Christmas Day 12/25/2000	14
Kensington Park	16
Montreux Jazz Festival — Detroit	17
Hagia Sophia	18
Mont St. Michel	19
Delphi	20
Menhir of Dol	21
Boreas	22
Persephone's Tale	23
Cassandra	24
Riding The Blue Sapphire Mountains	26
Pre-Columbian Figure, Detroit Institute of Arts	27
For John Cage	28
Armillaria bulbosa	30
A Song I Can Sing	31

Blues Song	32
Tattoos	33
Science Fiction Love Poem #1	34
Science Fiction Love Poem #2	35
Science Fiction Love Poem #3	36
Saturday in Port Huron, Michigan	37
Love Is	38
Ipperwash	39
The Call In The Night	40
Pt. Reyes	42
Waiting For The Snow	46
Four Short Poems	48
Meditation For A Full Moon	49
The Day We Buried R.B.	50
My Great-Grandmother Chana Lifszyc née Bromberg	53
The Remission	54
Prologue to a Divorce	55
When I Think Of Israel	56
One Afternoon	57
Late In The Evening	58
It Comes	59
For My Father	60
I Am	63
This Is What It's Like	64
The Rainstorm	66
Purple Asters	67

Hot Tea On A Summer Night

The stove's orange coils glow
Emanating unearthly light
And setting the pot to whistling
Another day passes
The summer turns on it's solstice
An incessant wheel
Throwing off roses, day lilies, stars
The night's secrets unfurl
Lissome fantasies, sweet reveries
Softly rustling dreams
All swirling
Over a sweet
Steeped cup
Of steaming tea

Waiting

Glasses clinking, burgers frying,
　and you
amidst the chattering voices of patrons
weaving your way about the tables
waiting

I'm waiting too
seated at the bar
with my book and my lunch
for you
in your soup-and-guacamole blotched pants
to stop and chat
between trays of glasses and hot food

Quick snatches of conversation,
　　from Pythagoras to prostatitis,
　　transcendental meditation and traveling
Longing for some conversatius non-interruptus
beyond the patrons impatient stares

Your cigarette in the ashtray
wreathes a veil of smoke
as you step off again
to gather plates
leaving me to wonder
what it would be like
to walk down the street
arm in arm
under the sun
Free to move together and apart
as the desire moved us
mingling spirit and spit
weaving our own dance
the ecstasy
of no longer waiting

A Book

You hand me a book and say
"Here, do you want this?"
A copy of Milan Kundera's
"The Unbearable Lightness of Being"
You have just moved
to a modernist aerie
on the 19th floor
Through the glass wall
the city sparkles
like so many jewels
scattered across a field
The Ambassador Bridge alight
like a delicate necklace
adorning the river
Boxes fill the room
their contents a mystery
even to you
But you find the Kundera
and offer it to me
saying you no longer want it
I take it home
and place it
on a pile of books
in my bedroom

Evening Sky

Evening sky
Fiery saffron clouds
reflect the parting sun
The city exhales
cool breezes
of car exhaust
and industrial fumes
Queen Anne's Lace and chicory
waist-high in vacant lots
Hollyhocks blazing pure colors
on tall stalks
startling carmines
dappled garnets
abandoned buildings
a rust-red backdrop
Sudden summer rain
rinses the quarter
Lightning arroyos
vein the sky
The twilight shudders
rattled by thunder

Cass Corridor Bar

Sitting around Third Street Saloon
Late at night
Watching old reruns of the Ed Sullivan show
When Dave the bartender thunders "What about
　me? What about my fifteen minutes of fame?
　Andy Warhol says everyone should have fifteen
　minutes of fame!"
And someone says "It's come and gone, Dave,
　I think you've missed it, it's come and gone."
"But what about the endorsements? What about
　the millions of dollars?"
"The check's in the mail, Dave, the check's
　in the mail."
Meanwhile, there's the Beatles singing
　"I love you yeah, yeah, yeah"
　while the girls in the audience
　scream and swoon, and there's Elvis,
　and there's a woman in a scant costume
　pulling a string of light bulbs
　out of a man's mouth, and another man
　　throwing knives.

Someone gets up to leave the bar and says
 "Long live the United States, man, best
 fucking constitution around."
Dave shakes his hand and says "We've got a
 few more years left anyway."
And we laugh, and Dave pats me on the back,
 and the man leaves and Dave says "I hope
 he paid his tab."
And I lean back and order another beer.
We all remember watching Ed, the Sunday night
 family ritual, the 'really big shews'
Dave does his Ed imitation, and we all laugh
 and say —
  "The check's in the mail, Dave,
   the check's in the mail."

The Bartender

Nightly you take your place behind the bar
Wearing your black vest
Like an old soldier
Stoop-shouldered, soft-bellied
Face lined like a map of every Detroit bar you've ever worked
You preside over the night like old St. Nick
Dispensing solvent gifts in icy glasses
No one's mug stays empty for long
Occasionally you even pour one for yourself
   an ample shot of sweet dark rum
Solicitous father, you greet me by name
  in the smoky red recesses of this neighborhood saloon
     and pour one more

Evening Conversation

Early spring
Evening conversation
Out of doors
Late into the night
The candle flame
Fanned by the cool breeze
Is burning low
Wax drips
A paraffin cascade

A Night On The Town
(in memory of Jim Gustafson)

I

That night we all went to the International Institute to see a dance performance. The walls were lined with glass showcases containing ethnic dolls and artifacts. After the show, you found an exquisite crown from Cambodia, and it was glittering with a thousand jewels and rose into a long tapered point. We knew it must be two thousand years old and priceless, and even though you knew it was wrong you slid open the glass door and removed it and placed it on your head, and we said you looked like a queen, and you said maybe now I can attract some men, and if they don't like me I'll lower my head and gore them. Then a man who worked there came over and said you shouldn't have done that, that's what the glass panes are for.

II

Next we went over to the corner bar, and when we walked in there was hardly anybody there except for the infamous Cass Corridor poet Jim Gustafson, and even though he didn't know us he recognized us right away and shouted out - "At last! Here they are! Three dangerous women!"

III

After a while we decided to go to another bar, and Jim Gustafson was there too, seated in the corner. It was 3 am when the bartender put on some evocative music and we decided to dance. Suddenly Jim Gustafson was up and out of his chair, arms outstretched, like some larger-than-life Lord of Misrule, all 348 pounds of him waltzing amongst us, his shorts trying to slip down around his knees, singing — "Goddesses! Goddesses! I've died and gone to green heaven!"

D.L.

This is how I'll always remember you —
   drunk, swaggering
   just finishing a conversation
   with a deranged woman
   in the party store
Brandishing your art like a sword
Lone hunter in a wood
Cape billowing in the still wind
She saw a wolf
There was none
but you concurred

Later, sitting in the car
reciting Irish poetry
reminiscing about mists and bogs
beard damp with beer
your spittle spattered the page
as you mispronounced the words
moved by ancestral memories
of forgotten ancient ways

Unruly and inappropriate as you are
 a stumbling boor
  intransigent bum
you never fail
to leave me
with a poem

Halloween Night

All the walls, grey
   as grey as old snow
In French — *neige gris*
A thousand plastic spiders glisten
   in the dark
They are plastic, yet alive nevertheless,
   everlasting
Pink skeletons ogle and stare, agog
while an ancient televisual oracle
   spews ludicrous pubescent fantasies
in pseudo sci-fi speak
In the movie
the women and spiders merge, mute
   and ferocious as Spanish dancers
while the men go mad and sputter insane jargon
   uttering science
And I am seated next to you, O Queen
on 50-cent chairs and bargain-basement tables
Welcome, welcome to the luciferous
   Nightmare Café

Christmas Day 12/25/2000

A bottle of cheap Yugoslavian wine will do
You snatched it out of the pantry
on our way to the party
The millennial Christmas
Festive as any other
but we don't even care
  — we're Jews!

Pagans, gamesters, queers and geeks
assemble to pass the evening
in mirthful merriment
You propose a game
where the rules never stay the same
everyone is enthralled
Flux is the hit of the party
Everyone can occupy themselves
deciphering the continuum
that constitutes the rules

Before we go
we plant a package
of fake rattlesnake eggs
to frighten the host
Alas, the buzz mechanism breaks
and we overhear the hostess
discoursing on its engineering flaws

After spice cookies, gingerbread, sugar drops
and wine in plastic cups
we continue to laugh and talk
as we drive home through the snow

Kensington Park

Walking the nature trails
at Kensington Park
off the winding path
near a shallow pond

Heavy-footed humans
with loud buffoon voices
frighten all the tadpoles
from their muddy abodes

   "Look, that one's sunning itself on a reed!"
   "That one has little back legs!"
   "That one's throat puffs out
      when he makes that sound!"
   "Where?"
   "There!"
   "Where?"
   "There!"

Amphibians
which came before reptiles
creatures of two worlds
We bid adieu
to these, our distant ancestors
and walk on

Montreux Jazz Festival – Detroit

The traffic
bumper-to-bumper
on Jefferson Avenue
snaking by The Fist
alongside Noguchi's plaza

People crowd the amphitheater
glowing faces
turned toward the sky
as jazz enlivens the night
like the lights
from the passing ships
gliding by
on the Detroit River

Ramsey Lewis' piano
weaves an aural tapestry
of grace
blessing this battered city

While nearby, the fountain
a tubular glistening ring
spews out a golden cloud of mist
that rains down
on the plaza
baptizing the children

[The Monument to Joe Louis, also known as The Fist, is a memorial located at Detroit's Hart Plaza. Hart Plaza in on the Detroit riverfront and was designed by Isamu Noguchi in 1978]

Hagia Sophia

Rose-hued cathedral
Church and mosque
Queen of Byzantium
You rise above
this overcrowded city
solid and majestic
red pillars hauled from Ephesus
your golden secrets
plastered and hidden
the human form
anathema to the conquering Turks
Saints, virgin, the lamb of God
Your Byzantine icons
glisten in the fading sun
Sophia, goddess of wisdom
Your temple still stands
in the heart of this pulsing city
testament to our eternal quest

Mont St. Michel

Man-made
Mountain of stone
Defying the sea
Narrow cobblestone streets
Labyrinthine wreaths
Spiraling upwards
To vast stone chambers
Moist grottoes
The Seven Stations of the Cross
Cathedral piercing the sky
Alabaster form
Gigantic and still
Sword raised to strike
Standing on the dragon
Death-bringer
Perfect, poised
So beautiful
You take my breath from me

Delphi

On a luxury bus
Gliding beneath the Mediterranean sun
past Parnassus, Thebes, and the fateful crossroads
   where Oedipus and Laius met
   to fulfill their inescapable destinies
Driving inexorably
to the center of the world
   the omphalos
   Delphi, Apollo's abode
To this day
the crowds still flock
to pay homage
to reconstructed pillars and treasuries
And the place where she sat
drunk on vapors and laurel leaves
   — the mad, demented Pythia
spewing forth prophecies
truths emanating
from the core of the earth
for the priests and interpreters
to tame for supplicant's ears
What did she think
as she bathed in the Castalian spring
amidst these craggy peaks
preparing herself to be taken by the god?
Throughout the ages
the unbearable truth
has always issued
from the mouths of madwomen

Menhir Of Dol

Here I stand
at the center of the world
Smooth, moss-covered
axis of stone

Here I have stood
since the beginning of time
in eloquent silence
A singing stone

Sun, moon, stars
all revolve around my song
Voice within the granite
heavy with time

Each year the corn
rises and falls
and the wheat
sways to my breath

Each night
I am consumed by the moon
yet at dawn
I still remain

It is said —
When I no longer stand
so shall the world
cease to be

Boreas

November hails
and Boreas leaves his abode
Before his approach
the chrysanthemums fade
the trees are stripped bare
He seeks the warm autumn sun
but it flees from him
and all turn away
Furious, alone
like a wounded beast
he howls throughout the night

Persephone's Tale

Before, everything was known
The calm, quiescent passage
of the days, gentle as sleep
amidst women's idle chatter
One day
traversing familiar ground
I saw, out of the corner of my eye
the radiant, dazzling bloom
  — blinding narcissus
Spellbound, I remember reaching out
Before I could grasp it
the ground shifted and cracked
opening beneath my feet
He did not have to take me
I stumbled and fell
tumbling into the abyss
Everything changed,
now strange and uncanny
Time and space congealed
No light, I had to see with my skin
Out of pity
I ate what was offered
the sweet and acrid seeds
of the god Hades' yield

Cassandra

I stood there proudly
When Apollo spat in my face
And didn't even flinch
Though it burned like acid
Etching into my skin
Then froze like ice
All my nerves went numb
Except my eyes
Which blazed
Like sky-blue suns

Throughout the journey
The story unfurled before me
Like Clytemnestra's carpet
I knew the ending
Before it had even begun

My eyes on fire
I cried out my prophecies
To the sea
Shrill syllables
Words with wings
That flapped above my head
Like gulls
Then disappeared

Beneath the king's embraces
My body dissolved into dust
Except for my eyes

My eyes

And all the while, nearby
Apollo laughing

No one heeds me
Nobody needs me

Exhausted
Truly cursed
Even I
No longer
Believe myself

Riding The Blue Sapphire Mountains

In the 12th century
the poetess Mahadevi
forsook the king
took leave of all propriety
to wander the countryside
unclad, god-crazy
reborn every minute
into the jasmine-scented embraces
of her moon-mad lord
riding the blue sapphire mountains
the milky way
raining down
like snow

Mahadevi, this day and age
is no place
for a deliriously naked dakini
to walk the street
in blissful spirit-copulation
with the Lord of Dance

But, inviolable and unconcealed
I know
that if any man
ever
tried to touch you
his hands would
turn to stone

Pre-Columbian Figure, Detroit Institute Of Arts

You seem strangely out of place
in your new sanctuary
Crouching on a pedestal
in this dimly-lit gallery
like a wise old frog
your wooden face
wrinkles scored deep as furrows
hands grasping a tray
to hold offerings or incense for the gods
So animated, I half-expect
you to speak as I approach
to see smoke emanating
from your nostrils or your ears
Are you a god or a gnome?
Or someone's wizened grandfather doll?
Whoever you are
I know that you are crafty and obstinate
and would just as soon mislead and mystify
as properly prophesize my destiny

For John Cage

A piano, prepared
The strings
stretched and muted
with wood and gum
A complete percussive orchestra
Melange of sounds

This is a happening
A break with the past
Musicians play tin plates, pans
a kitchen cacophony
Collection of found sounds

Next, on the violin
we will play the stars
just to prove we can
A celestial symphony
a notable space

In the woods
of North Carolina
you wander, stepping lightly
hunting for mushrooms
Fleshy fungi
turning the forests' detritus
back into earth

a mycological decomposition
a saprophytic song
soft supple silence
of nature's processes
unseen and inaudible
a gathering of muted tones

If you have taught us anything
you have taught us
that the human heart
cannot be analyzed
like a classical sonata

Lanky anarchist
you compose for the stars
and they respond
extemporaneously
in stellar silence
which is brilliant
and miraculous

Armillaria bulbosa

Discovered
Between Crystal Falls and Marquette
By a perspicacious scientist
Made the morning papers, and The New York Times
Larger than anyone imagined
Filaments forty acres across
Older than the redwoods
Or the twisted bristlecone pines
Armillaria bulbosa
Stump mushrooms
Silently expanding
Since the last Ice Age
Feeding on the forests' detritus
Occasionally poking above the soil
Honey mushrooms
Patiently populating the UP in perpetuity

[UP refers to the Upper Peninsula of Michigan]

A Song I Can Sing

I'd like to write a song that I can sing
I'd like to write a song that I can sing
Don't have to be a pretty thing
I've always lived my life on the wing
I'd like to write a song that I can sing

Sunday, grey day Sunday, rainy day
Driving down the freeway, on my way
A line of pigeons perching on a ledge
I've always lived my life out on the edge

I don't really mind being alone
It's easier to make it on my own
Memories of days gone by, once you loved me,
  thought I'd die
When you told me got to say good-bye

That was a long time ago
If I close my eyes I still see your shadow
Did you really hold me close at night?
Your beauty makes me curse my sight
Sweet promises made so long ago
Words dissolve like late-spring snow

I'd like to write a song that I can sing
I'd like to write a song that I can sing
You could have stayed, I'd treat you like a king
But freedom seemed a much better thing.

Blues Song

Well I know a man
goes out drinking every day
Well I know a man
goes out drinking every day
From sunup 'til sundown
that man drinks his life away

He's all dressed in leather
with a head of fine red hair
He's all dressed in leather
with a head of fine red hair
When he goes out at night
all the women stare

When he comes round to see me
can't even hold his head up high
When he comes round to see me
can't even hold his head up high
But when I lay my body down
he makes me want to die

He leaves me in the morning
has no more thoughts about me
He leaves me in the morning
doesn't give a damn about me
He leaves me to myself
just like that empty bottle of whiskey

Tattoos

Proliferating on your back
In vivid shades and hues
Luxuriant savage orchids
Profusion of tropical birds
A gorgeous arboretum
Hothouse of blue tattoos
An epidermal menagerie
Cloistered chimerical zoo

Science Fiction Love Poem #1

From this small window
round as a fish eye
or a diminutive moon
I peer into the atmosphere
expanse of empty space
toward our nearest neighbor
aboriginal button
the alpha abode
gleaming green and blue
Your glittering instruments
have vaulted me
to this rugged world
to take root
like a foreign spore
Together we labor
to make water and air
and take evening strolls
through craggy canals
and coral clouds
O my love,
I'd follow you
to whatever strange galaxy
your love would take me

Science Fiction Love Poem #2

Darling, how I long for the nights
when, breaking free of gravity
we careen between the stars
like a drunken comet
Enclosed in our own world
your hand at the wheel
superconductors spinning
brushing the edges
of this
our known galaxy
Lapping the light
of the Milky Way
soaring between Orion's legs
tweaking Pegasus' tail
O my fellow traveler
time's joy
knows no boundaries
when I am strapped beside you
hurtling towards the sun

Science Fiction Love Poem #3

Child of Venus
Son of the morning star
I haven't been able to escape
your gravitational pull
the protean spectrum
of your enchantment
Eyes radiant as Aldebaran
Skin gleaming like burnished cobalt
Hair dark as an ebony penumbra
O empyrean boy
There's none to compare
to your quicksilver beauty
Could you ever cast
your luminous glances
toward a quiescent terrestrial
an earthly woman
shackled to land?

Saturday In Port Huron, Michigan

    Saturday in Port Huron
        gone fishing
off the tip   of the thumb
    returning sun-burned
       and rested

      That evening
       your eyes
          touched my skin
      like fire

Love Is

Love is
a deep well
that makes no promises
It catches
It cajoles
It takes you
to places
you've never been
It catches you
unawares
Sly thief
Love will pick your pocket
take you for a joy-ride
then leave you
at the side of the road
wondering under the stars

Ipperwash

The sun goes down at Ipperwash
Great Lake swallowing the day
We have crossed the Blue Water Bridge
Come to read on the beach
I read the thin bands of sand
Flakes of chert, dead butterflies
A handful of shells to amuse you
A twisted stick
How much more time do we have?
One month? Two?
You left me once
at the dunes
on the shore
of Silver Lake
To wander past driftwood and gulls
It was the end of May
Spring winds blowing cold
I know now what I knew then
You left me once, you'll do it again

The Call In The Night

Sweet, nearly forgotten
dear one.
The phone rings
in the middle of the night
and I think
its the death of a loved one.

But its you
settling delicately
like a pleasant dream
or a phantasmic butterfly
ethereal colors dazzling
calling from Three Rivers
and its like the months and years
have never passed
Memories, yesterdays
suddenly spring up today
and time dissolves
as only it can
when kindred spirits speak

Love me
with your illusions and fantasies
with your might-have-beens
with your should-haves
Love me
with confessions
that you think of me
always
that you should have never
let me go

Your spirit
awakening my spirit
As it always has
We will always be
   as we were
Dancing in some other
   ethereal space
Music, vibrations, ecstasies

A fabulous butterfly
   alighting unexpectedly
Your colors dazzling
Alight
and sip one drop
Talk yourself
to the edge of dawn
Turn, touch me
And then, lightly
Once again
fly away

Pt. Reyes

Awakening
to morning mist
tall trees overhead
   arching over shady
   foliage-covered grove
Pitching our tent in the ferns
We slept on the earth
   huddled to her breast
   throughout the night
The joyous birds and grey light
diffusing through the damp mist
   awakened us
We were in California
near the ocean
blue Pacific

That day we were
   the first ones
   down the path
Four miles to the coast
Lugging heavy packs
   then hiding them in the bush
Wanting to walk free, unburdened
We came upon some deer
   swift, delicate creatures
   brown-tan
And then a pure white one
   with a full rack
   of ebony antlers

and his brown-black friend
moving back slowly
  into the forest
  as we approached
We stopped at a cool brook
  along the way
its destination
  the same
  as ours

Almost noon
The forest opened out
into rolling brown hills
one folding out onto another
Cresting to ridges
The thin path winding
  gently upwards
  towards the sky
It was then we glimpsed our first
  view of her
A vast, turquoise jewel
  between the hills
Only a short hike now
  to Arch Rock

Atop high crumbling cliffs
covered with strange succulent plants
The place where earth and water
  meet sun and sky
The crossroads of the elements

Offshore
   a solid monolith of rock
   deserted by receding cliffs
   populated with seabirds
     cormorants and gulls
Dark hawks circling overhead
   with terrible fierce beaks
Pelicans skimming alongside the cliff
Bright sun shining
   on naked bodies
Your kiss, your touch
Pressing me to the earth

Another path
Winding down into the gully
   now swift brook
   rushing home
   dancing over stones
   amidst bright yellow blossoms
Damp niche in the cliff
   stone bandshell
   God's thumbprint
Green ferns springing from the wall

Down on the beach
   grains of sand beneath our feet
   cold whipping wind
   starfish clinging to the rocks
     soft colors, soft hands
Crabs scurrying between fallen slates
   clack-clack

So much life in the tide pool.
And close offshore
at first looking like a piece of driftwood
  a sleek seal
  head emerging
  from the surf
  kindred spirit

Beneath the cliffs
  leading to the sea
Two arches, low and wide
We had to crawl underneath
Past swollen seaweed-fruit
  knees in wet sand
  now on the other side
  sun and wind
  bleaching to bone
Down on the beach
  in a small cave
  beneath the cliffs
Arching over you
Your salty brine foaming onto my lips
  milk of life
  sea of pleasure
Resting my head on your thighs
  giving thanks
  for such fullness
  for the sea, for life
  for our love

Waiting For The Snow

Sunday afternoon
A series of improvised errands
The Wine Shoppe on Orchard Lake Road
Aromatic heady Belgian beer
Spargolo Sangiovese from Toscana
and a golden-white ice wine from Germany
which the proprietor gives us, gratis

Next the Italian brother's market
Browsing amidst large aloes, pies, biscotti
   elegant elongated French breads peeking
   from paper wrappers
The cart brimming with fresh vegetables
a pear-shaped butternut squash
Shimmering pink blossoms of cyclamen
hovering above the oranges
like pale flames

We thought winter was over
But snow will be coming tonight
Late February yet to have its say
To strains of Billie Holiday singing —
   "everything ends too soon, too soon...."

Laden with packages
The cat greets us at the door
Home before the first flakes
drift from the sky
Imbibing wine from stemless glasses
Awaiting the midnight hush
The silent relentless blanketing
Waiting for the snow

Four Short Poems

I

Upon sighting the man
the white egret starts
and then takes flight

II

Before the storm breaks
the white egrets circle
above the reeds

III

Canadian geese and their young
forage in the tall grass
The rainstorm does not perturb them

IV

At the sound of thunder
the egrets circle above
Below, the bullfrogs laugh

Meditation For A Full Moon

On the night of a full moon
Sit by the shore of a lake
Be still
Be silent
Wait

Bathe in the light of the moon
Listen to voices of wild geese and swans
Be still
Be silent
Wait

The Day We Buried R.B.

You had it all —
intoxicating beauty, glamour, talent
the career of an itinerant musician
dancing throughout the nights
on the beaches of the Caribbean
and the love of beautiful blond women
who loved you like life itself.

And yet it wasn't enough

How can we, who remain,
possibly even understand
what drove you
to end it all
in the anonymity
of a randomly chosen
Florida hotel room?

Certainly not your two remaining sisters,
bereft and uncomprehending
Nor your infirm elderly father
tottering with his cane
whom you presumed to blame

We gathered
on this late March afternoon
spring barely gaining a toehold
before death's cold hand
had its say
on this grey overcast day

Slightly bruised yet still lovely
ensconced in a white lace shroud
Your still apparent beauty
in your plain wood coffin
an affront
to anyone who dared to gaze

First your sister
downed in a sordid blaze of bullets
Bigger-than-life denouement
for a suburban Jewish girl
defiant in her addictions.

Then your mother, survivor,
child of the Holocaust,
poetess and wild soul,
gone in her own time.
If my mother were alive to say it,
she'd say 'at least she didn't live
to see this'.

But we have,
our mother's heirs
wounded women
with our dogs and our cats,
our children and husbands,
our books and poems and songs.
Sticking it out
Still holding on

Your funeral,
the day before Passover

I leave the sodden cemetery
with a sister of my own
to labor the evening away
I'll make a Sephardic charoset
with dates, almonds, cinnamon, vanilla and wine.
Sweet mortar of the slaves we once were
to be consumed at the family Seder
and blended with maror —
the bitter herbs

The bitter reproach of your passing
by your own hand
Your sister, barely able to see through her tears,
without even the consolation of being able to say
good-bye.

We were all once slaves in Egypt,
and then we were free.
Free to own our bodies,
to sing and celebrate,
to dance on beaches,
love whom and when we could.
Free to celebrate and despair.
And free to choose.

[Charoset is a dish made of fruits, nuts and wine and eaten at the Passover Seder. It is meant to recall the mortar used by the Israelite slaves in ancient Egypt. Maror are bitter herbs eaten at the Passover Seder. The Seder is the ritual of retelling the story of the liberation of the Israelites from slavery in ancient Egypt]

My Great-Grandmother Chana Lifszyc née Bromberg

Great-grandmother
Your daughter told me
you were a lousy cook
After arising at dawn
and seeing your six children off to school
you prepared the evening meal
and placed it in the oven
and there is would sit
all day
while you,
perched on top
of the kitchen table
beneath the only lamp in the house
would sit all day
and read —
   Dostoevsky, Aleichem, Tolstoy
So, great-grandmother
Every class I take
is for you
Every book I read,
for you
Every poem I write —
for you.
From the ashes
of your unmarked grave
at Treblinka
the light of your spirit rises
to inspire my life

The Remission

Your recovery, though temporary
is nothing short of miraculous
A resurrection of sorts
And I can almost envision you well
This nightmare of hospitalizations
   IVs, chemo, X-rays, debilitation
fading like a child's huge fears
evaporating at daybreak

Your friends, gathered over a lifetime
come by in a continuous parade
You hold court
ensconced in your bed
like an honored guest
We visit for long hours, converse, convene
   eat sweets

Last week the doctor gave you six months
But today he came by and said
"I cannot offer you a cure,
but I can tell you,
today
you are not dying."

The laughter spills out
into the hallway of Hem-Onc
Conviviality holding death's spectre
at bay

Prologue To A Divorce

Dense thickets of arguments
Entanglement of thorns
A frightened witch
Dances with a voiceless ghost

Briers. Dead roses. Lies.
An abandoned garden
Foundering marriage
Within your unhappiness
We grew like weeds

When I Think Of Israel

When I think of Israel
I think of my father
As a child
Standing on the beach in Tel Aviv
Holding a balloon
Dreaming the soccer ball
That danced between his feet
Would take flight
Like the moon
The moon reflected on the sea
Where he danced and sang with his friends —
   "we don't want to go to sleep
   we want to go crazy"
The long summers
   at Kibbutz Dorot, Tzorah, and Zhamadiyah
Harvesting grapes
And three years in the army
When I think of Israel
I think of my father
My father
Whose soul will always belong
To the land of Israel.

One Afternoon

There is a clear unobstructed view
from the roof of the apartment
Several planes
like great, gliding birds
slice through the sky
My parents are unaware
that I am here
Sight-line above the city
the wind caressing my hair

One by one the planes
toss out their strange confetti
They revel in this wedding
of sound and destruction
Tel Aviv was bombed
by the Italian Air Force
in 1940 and 1941
The war we barely fled
arriving at our doorstep

Late In The Evening

I sit, late in the evening
among my books arrayed on shelves
and some of them are yours
passed on to me
when you passed on.

I know which book came from each of you.

In the silence of this night
alone, I'm struck
by how impoverished I am
by your passing

What am I
but a remnant
of your lives and deeds.

It Comes

It comes.
Slowly, surreptitiously
it sidles, sneaks, sulks
and you sense it
nearing,
It comes from behind
but you turn, and look ahead
Relentless burglar
it takes until its taken
everything you have
  — strength, sense, sight
    and pride
Like Lear
stripped bare in the storm
lashed
Its a howling
this demise

For My Father

> — *Father would ask:*
> *"What am I going to do with you?*
> *You're a dreamer*
> *and shouldn't be let out*
> *into the world...."*
>> — from the poem "Father" in "Portrait Without Frames"
>> by Lev Ozerov

The time I remember
seeing you happiest
was at Camp Tamarack
circa 1972
performing
playing music — Israeli, Yiddish —
with a trio of your friends.
Music was always so dear
and close to your heart —
Chava Alberstein, Leo Fuld,
and the marvelous cantors of yore.
Three years before my 16th birthday
my mother unceremoniously
evicted you.
Afterwards I dreamt
you were a ghost
occasionally returning
to haunt the family.
On that birthday
(was it a sunny or cloudy day in April?)
you took me to
The Holiday Inn
on Telegraph and Ten Mile Road,

a tall cylindrical tower
clad in mirrors
reflecting the sky.
There we sat
in the revolving restaurant
on the top floor
across from each other,
rotating in silence.
I was never given to girlish chatter
and you appeared stricken, mute.
Was it with grief, still?
Or did I appear as strange and inaccessible to you
as you to me?
How far away you seemed
despite sitting right across from me.
Like the ghost in my dreams.
It took several decades
before conversation began
to flow between us,
reminiscing about your youth
in Israel — the Mediterranean,
the kibbutzim, the one-room
family apartment
illuminated by a single bulb.
Finally, when I no longer
needed anything
you found a way to have something to give.
And what did I know of your needs
throughout those long decades?
Nothing.
Apparently nothing.
Then, in your final months
the conversations became shorter,

the music of your voice dwindling
to only a few words,
the streams and currents of conversation
slowing to a trickle.
I would ask — "How was your day, what did you do?"
And you would reply — "I can't remember."
As you were slipping away
I wondered if you were angry with me,
or depressed, if illness was stealing your thoughts,
or perhaps a mixture of the above.
Once again,
like the door to a singular room
closing.
Enclosed and distant.
Again, inaccessible.

I Am

I am
Fragments of memories
A stolen butterfly pin
A Venus flytrap
Sunning itself by the window
In a jar
Childhood nights
The 16 mm projector
Old Chaplin films flickering
On the living room wall
Before you left us
Were made to leave
I am still learning
How not to abandon you

This Is What It's Like

So this is what it's like

The late afternoon sun
Striking the brass knob
Of the closet door on which
Hangs the small burlap square
With a diminutive skewed heart you cross-stitched
Out of black and yellow threads
Balanced above the inscription of the word 'love'.

You so enjoyed
The arts and crafts days
Sitting at the table
With the women
Working with your hands
Making an object to show and share
To place somewhere in your room
That's what it came to
A man who once ran a company
Obtained grants, hobnobbed with governors
Now making trinkets in his twilight years
Using thread, beads, paint and wood
A time, I suppose, that comes to us all

I suppose it broke up the days

It was that one time, in your room
You in your recliner
Me annoyed with you, you annoyed with me
I cannot even remember the reason we quarreled
But I must have assumed we had
All the time in the world to do so

It was then you said to me
  — "One day I won't even be here anymore"

And then that day came to pass
And other days followed

And this is what it's like
When you're not here anymore
One day after another
You're not here anymore

The Rainstorm

The day's work done
Late afternoon storm clouds
break the summer's heat

Rain falling
straight and hard
battering the asphalt

Maybe now I can think

There's somewhere
I'm supposed to be
and its not here

Like the humidity
rising from the street
a question hangs
in the air —
Then where?

And when
did I lose
myself?

Purple Asters

Unexpected
A swatch of purple
on the edge
of a schoolyard
An unruly cluster of asters
like a bruise
Signaling summer's end

A marker of the turning season
Darker skies, cooler nights
This violaceous flare
stands as sentry
to time's passing

About the Author

Deborah Hochberg is from Detroit, Michigan, and studied at Wayne State University She is a musician, a naturalist, and a nurse practitioner. She has previously written about film for the *Detroit Metro Times*.

www.ingramcontent.com/pod-product-compliance
Lightning Source LLC
Chambersburg PA
CBHW022108040426

42451CB00007B/187